PEOPLE WHO HELP US

Police Officer

Alison Cooper and Diana Bentley

Photographs by
Chris Fairclough

People Who Help Us

Ambulance Crew
Bus Driver
Firefighter
Flight Attendant
Lifeboat Crew
Nurse
Police Officer
Train Driver
Vet

Designer: David Armitage

First published in 1990 by
Wayland (Publishers) Ltd
61 Western Road, Hove
East Sussex, BN3 1JD, England

© Copyright 1990 Wayland (Publishers) Ltd

British Library Cataloguing in Publication Data
Bentley, Diana
   Police officer.
   1. Great Britain. Police
   I. Title II. Cooper, Alison III. Fairclough, Chris
   IIII. Series
   363.2'0941

ISBN 1–85210–850–9

Typeset by L. George & R. Gibbs, Wayland
Printed and bound in Belgium by Casterman S.A.

Contents

Words that are <u>underlined</u> appear
in the glossary on page 30.

Bob is a police officer.

Have you ever met a police officer?
Police officers do all kinds of different jobs.
Bob is a <u>community police officer</u>. He helps
the people who live in his special area of
the town.

<u>Inspector</u> Holmes is in charge of this group of officers. Every day he tells them what jobs they have to do. This is called a briefing.

This is the police station control room.

Some officers work in the control room. They answer the phone calls. They put all the details on to their computers. Then they tell the officers on <u>patrol</u> where to go and what to do.

A school <u>caretaker</u> has just called them.
She thinks there may be a <u>burglar</u> inside her
school. The school's radio is missing.

Bob goes to the school.

Each police officer has a different area of the town to look after. The school is in Bob's area. He goes there with some other officers. One of the officers has a specially trained dog. This officer is called a dog handler.

The dog handler tells Bob he will take the dog into the school first, in case the burglar is still inside. The burglar might be dangerous.

Whose fingerprints are these?

This officer is trying to find out where the burglar got into the school. He dusts some powder on to the window.

Look! Now you can see some fingerprints on the window. Perhaps they were made by the burglar. The police will make a <u>record</u> of them.

This is a mounted police officer.

Mounted police officers use horses to patrol large areas like parks.

Bob meets the mounted police officer in a
park near the school. He tells the officer to
look out for the burglar.

The police <u>track</u> the burglar.

The police use dogs to find people who are lost or hiding. The dog sniffs the ground. It can tell if someone has been walking there.

The police dog has found a man hiding!
WPC Pam chases after him. The letters
WPC before Pam's name mean 'Woman
Police Constable'.

WPC Pam <u>arrests</u> the man.

The man is frightened of the police dog.
Pam puts <u>handcuffs</u> on the man. This is to
stop him from running away. They take him
to the police station in a police car.

The man is charged.

Pam tells the man why she has arrested him. This is called reading the charge. The man will go to <u>court</u> in a few days' time. A <u>judge </u>will decide if he should be punished.

The police make a record of the man's fingerprints. Everyone has different fingerprints. If these are the same as the ones the police found at the school, it will help them to <u>prove</u> that this man was the burglar.

Bob receives a radio message.

The message is from the control room.
There is a traffic jam at a crossroads in
Bob's area. Bob gets the traffic moving
again. He uses arm signals to tell the drivers
when they can go.

Bob checks the computer.

Bob is back at the station. He has just had his lunch. Before he goes back on patrol, he checks the computer. It tells him what has been happening in the town during the morning.

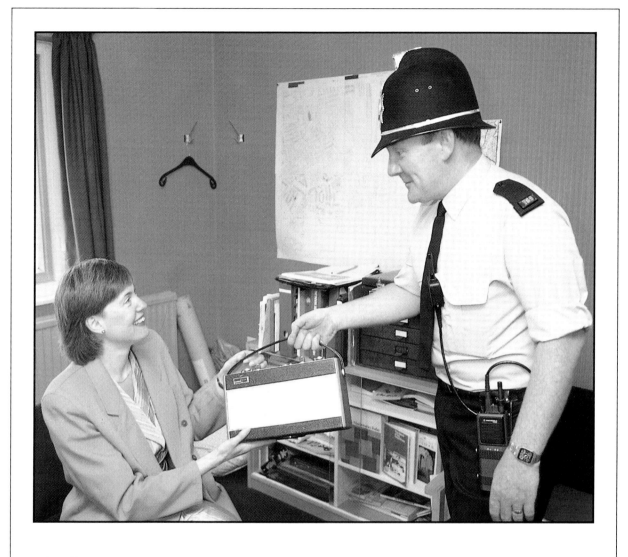

Bob returns the stolen radio.

This is the radio that the man was carrying
when he was arrested. Bob takes it to the
headteacher. It is the school's radio. She is
pleased to get it back!

Bob helps two children.

Jagdeep and Pradeep have been home for lunch. Bob stops the traffic so that they can cross the road near their school.

Bob visits an old lady.

Bob visits the old people in his area. He makes sure that none of them are ill, and that their homes are safe. They like to talk to him.

Bob gives a talk at a school.

Bob visits schools too. He tells the children how to be safe when they are playing outside. He tells them not to talk to strangers, and never to get into their cars.

Percy talks to the children too! He is a little police car. Bob can make him talk using a special control box. Has Percy ever visited your school?

Bob has finished work for today.

Bob goes back to the police station.
Inspector Holmes asks all his officers to tell
him what they have done during the day.
A different group of officers will take over
now. There are always some officers on
duty – even during the night.

Bob has a game of <u>snooker</u> with Pam
before he goes home. He likes snooker –
but he hopes Pam is not going to win!

Glossary

Arrests   Stops someone and takes them to the
   police station.

Burglar   Someone who breaks into a building to
   steal things.

Caretaker   Someone who looks after a building,
   for example, a school.

Community police officer   An officer who helps
   people living in a particular area.

Court   A place where a person who may have
   broken the law is sent. The police tell the judge
   why they have arrested that person and the
   judge decides if the person should be punished.

Handcuffs   A pair of metal rings joined by a
   chain. One ring is fastened to a police officer
   and one to the person being arrested.

Inspector   A police officer who is in charge of
   other officers.

Judge   Someone who decides what
   punishment to give to people who have
   broken the law.

Patrol   Walk or drive round an area to make sure
   no one is causing trouble, or to see if anyone
   needs help.

<u>Prove</u> Show something is true.

<u>Record</u> Write something down, for example what an object looks like.

<u>Snooker</u> A game played on a large table. Players try to push coloured balls into pockets using special sticks called cues.

<u>Track</u> Follow someone.

Books to read

The Police Force Fiona Corbridge (Wayland, 1985)

Police Station Andrew Langley (Franklin Watts, 1983)

Police Woman Brenda Clarke (Franklin Watts, 1984)

Safety on the Road Dorothy Baldwin and Claire Lister (Wayland, 1987)

Safety When Alone Dorothy Baldwin and Claire Lister (Wayland, 1987)

Index

Acknowledgements

The authors and publishers would like to thank the following for their help in the preparation of this book: The Chief Constable, West Yorkshire Police Force; the Community Involvement Unit, Bradford Central Police Station; the headteacher, staff and pupils of Bowling Park First School and Mrs. D. Harwood.